Ms. Loops presents...

Handwriting Clues Club Books

Book 1
Clues to Find in Cursive & Print

Book 2
A-Z Dictionary of Clues

Book 3
A-Z Clues of Iggy... as found by Peony

Join the Handwriting Clues Club of
adventurous people who become clues finders!

Ms. Loops Presents...

Handwriting Clues Club – Book 2

A–Z Dictionary of Clues

by Judy Kaplan

(aka Ms. Loops)

Drawing of Ms. Loops by

Wayne Ramirez

Drawing of Ms. Loops by Wayne Ramirez.

Printed by KDP - https://kdp.amazon.com
ISBN: 978-1-957373-03-4 (Paperback)
ISBN: 978-1-957373-05-8 (Mobi)

Printed by Ingram Sparks - https://www.ingramspark.com
ISBN: 978-1-957373-10-2 (Hardback)
ISBN: 978-1-957373-04-1 (Epub)

Library Catalog Dewey Classification # - 155.2'82
Kaplan, Judy.
1. Graphology   2. Writing   3. Handwriting Analysis
I. Title.   II. Series.   III. Wayne Ramirez, illustrator

Judy Kaplan Books

JudyKaplanBooks.com

Acknowledgements

Thank you to the highly knowledgeable and professional handwriting analysts at these organizations:
American Handwriting Association Foundation
ahafhandwriting.org
American Association of Handwriting Analysts
aahahandwriting.org
International Grapho-Analysis Association
igas.com
Your courses, workshops, certification programs, and mentoring have been a thorough and enlightening education in handwriting analysis.

Thank you Linda Larson for your remarkably detailed evaluation of the information in this book.

Thank you to my family and friends for their incredible support, encouragement and patience throughout my writing.

Thank you to Wayne Ramirez for his wonderful depictions of my characters Ms. Loops, Iggy & Peony.

Author Information

Judy Kaplan has held a life-long fascination for writing, handwriting, and books. After a 27 year career as a High School Library Media Specialist, she began a second career as a Handwriting Analyst. She has Handwriting Analyst Certifications from both ahafhandwriting.org and igas.com. She specializes in personality and compatibility profiles. She created the Handwriting Clues Club series of books to promote understanding and compatibility in an easy, fun, and informative format for all ages.

GLOSSARY
of letter parts

Baseline - ⌊baseline⌋ is the ⌊real line⌋ or
⌊imaginary line⌋ that letters are written on.

x-height - is the height of ↕x or any letter without an
ascender and descender ↕aceimnorsuvwxz

Letter Zones -

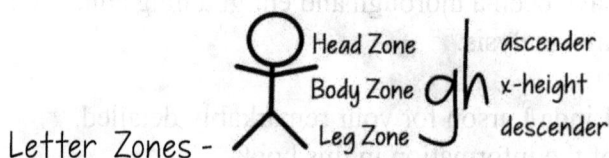

Upper zone ↑bdfhklt is called the head zone or ascender.
This part of a letter shows how a person thinks about
ideas.

Middle zone →ghx is called body zone or x-height.
This part of a letter shows how a person communicates
and interacts with others.

Lower zone ↘gjpqy is called leg zone or descender.
This part of a letter shows how a person does their
physical actions.

Backbone or also called Stem - the tall line that supports the rest of the letter:

⭥E ⭥I ⭥H ⭥K ⭥T ⭥A ⭥Z ⭥b d⭥ ⭥f ⭥h ⭥k

Arm or Leg - a line attached to the Backbone. Arms are the middle & top strokes: E⭰ F⭰ K← k←

Legs are the bottom strokes: E⭩ K⭩ k⭩ and the descender below the baseline ↳ gjpqy

Crossbar - the line that crosses a Stem: f← T⭦

or connects two Stems: A←H←. t← is called a t-bar.

Swash - an extended decorative stroke on a letter:

⌐A ⌐M ⌐Y

Flourish - a swirly showy stroke: ↘A ↘N⭦ L⭩

Beak - the horizontal stroke that starts on the left side of the Stem: ↗B ↗D ↗P ↗R

Graphology - The study of learning clues shown in handwriting. People who analyze clues in handwriting for more understanding of the person are called Graphologists or Handwriting Analysts.

LETTER MEANINGS A - Z

These meanings always apply:

Narrow letters show the person is narrow-minded. They stick to what's familiar, don't want to extend themselves to new ways of thinking, and keep their feelings to themselves.

Wide letters show the person is broad-minded. They are very tolerant, outgoing, and can easily be gullible.

Square letters show the person is logical and practical. They enjoy building and construction projects.

Straight lines show liking to follow a straight step by step plan. When writing has a lot of straight lines the person sticks straight to their plan and dislikes anything that gets in the way of moving straight ahead.

Angles show the person's mind is pointing straight to problems and their solutions. When writing is loaded with angles, it shows they are critical, impatient, insistent on doing things their way, and quick to anger.

Curves show a friendly nature. When you see writing that is mostly curves the person is yielding, nurturing, gentle, and wants to please.

1

Closed loops show feelings, imagination, and personal thoughts held inside. When writing has many loops it shows the person is always thinking about something personal inside their own head, even when they're listening to what others are talking about.

Tall ascenders show an idealistic mind. The person thinks a lot about ideas and ideals involving philosophy, ethics, religion, science, or global issues.

When d or t ascenders are over 3 times the x-height d_x or t_x, the person's thinking is about how great they are and how they deserve much more attention for it than they get.

Long descenders show long lasting determination to stick to their activity for very long periods of time to get their task done.

Short descenders show they only spend a short time on tasks and give up fast.

x-height tallest, meaning when the body zone is the tallest of the 3 zones, shows the person's main focus is on their everyday practical matters and their social interactions with others.

Capitals that are Simple and Clear Show the Person is Intelligent, Efficient and Direct.

Capitals that are Extra Large show the person Wants to Appear Extra Important.

Capitals that are Extra Fancy show the person Wants to Appear Extra Impressive.

Light pressure shows the person has low physical energy and has a poor memory. They have a gentle nature, they avoid confrontation whenever possible, and they need rests in between physical activities. They also easily forgive and forget.

Heavy pressure shows the person has strong long-lasting physical energy and a strong long-lasting memory. They have an insistent and forceful personality. It's extremely hard for them to forgive and forget.

Slants can be ↑vertical↑, ↗right↗, or ↖left↖. They show how a person controls their emotions.

↑↓vertical slant is straight up & down. They keep their emotions under control at all times, rarely show if they are upset or angry, and stay objective in an emergency.

↗ right slant leans right ↗. They naturally lean towards others, are openly friendly, and show when they are upset.

The far right slant person can't control their feelings, gets upset quickly, and needs a lot of calming down.

↖ left slant leans left ↖. They control their feelings by holding them back and avoiding having to talk about their feelings or personal life until they are comfortable with the other person.

The far left slant person controls their feelings by staying alone when possible. They can be friendly but does not want to talk about themselves. They have trouble trusting anyone.

Variable slant is when slant shifts a lot ↖↗. The person with big shifts in slant has feelings that shift a lot and that they can't control. They are moody and unpredictable.

The person with small shifts in slant has small shifts in their feelings that they can usually control.

Clear space inside and between letters shows the person can think clearly and make good decisions.

T o o m u c h s p a c e b e t w e e n l e t t e r s shows the person has trouble keeping their thoughts connected. They lose track of all the different things they need to consider to make good decisions.

Writing that stays steady along the baseline shows a person who keeps a steady focus on tasks.

Bouncy writing that jumps up and down on the baseline shows the person has a hard time staying focused.

CONFUSED SPACE Overlapping letters shows confused thinking space. The person can't keep their thoughts clearly separated to think of any of them clearly. Lots of overlapping OVERLAPPING in the writing shows the person's thinking is a constant jumble. It's easy for them to get frustrated.

Look at the whole writing and gather many different clues. If a clue appears often, then the person does that often. If a clue just appears once, it could be their arm changed position at that moment. The more clues you find, the more you will understand about yourself and the people around you.

a a

a is a body zone →*a*← circle letter. The circle shape
represents the person's mouth. Body zone circle letters
a c o show how a person talks and what's going
on in their mind when they communicate with others.

a- A clear inside circle shows they speak honestly.
They feel they have nothing to hide.

a - A hook or line inside the circle shows they are
hiding something that's on their mind. They will be
evasive and not talk about that particular thing.

a - A loop on the right side of the circle shows
they have private thoughts they want to keep to
themselves. It can be secrets or simply personal
matters.

a - Very big loops show the person's feelings about
their private thoughts or secrets has inflated to the
point of upset or fear. It's on their mind a lot.

a - Loop on the left side shows there is some truth
about themselves they don't want to admit. It's locked
away in their mind, but keeping anything hidden keeps
them from being completely open in what they say.

α - Left & right loops that overlap shows overlapping private thoughts and secrets has their thinking confused. They can't keep the truth straight and easily lie to protect all they are hiding.

ɑ - Open circle shows they like to talk a lot.

a - Closed circle shows they only talk when needed. They also can be trusted not to tell another person's secret.

A - Caved-in crossbar shows they don't hold to firm goals.

A - High crossbar shows they are ambitious and will take risks to get more notice.

A - Low crossbar shows they have low ambitions and don't expect or try to get noticed.

A - Round top instead of a point shows they keep thoughts private and take their time making a decision.

ℓ b

b is a good letter to see a person's business ability.

First the stem goes to the head zone ↗ℓ ↗b for ideas. Then the body zone circle ℓ← b← shows how they make their decisions.

l b - This person has tall head idealistic ideas that shows they are also interested in philosophical, social or environmental concerns beyond what is practical for their current or business needs.

l b - This person has moderate height head thinking that sticks closer to practical ideas including social issues that are practical for their business or current purposes.

l D -This person's short head thinking sticks only to practical ideas for their current needs.

l G - Circle open on top shows they are open to other people's ideas & influence.

b b - Circle closed on top shows they stick to their own thinking and are closed to influence from others.

l b - Loop on top of circle shows they feel an emotional investment in their work. They have a personal belief or feeling that adds to their desire to do it.

l b - Circle very wide shows they are gullible and easily fooled by others.

b l - Letters up on a pedestal shows egotism. They believe they belong on a pedestal and expect others to look up to them.

b ℬ - Snail curls show they are self-centered and often selfish. Business decisions will only be based on what's personally best for them.

ℬ- Larger upper section shows they have an inflated ego that is bigger than their lower circle which is their business practical common sense. They make decisions more on feeding their ego than on common sense.

B - Lower section larger shows they are most concerned with what's practical. They make decisions on good business common sense.

ℬ - Wide loop stem shows an inflated ego that will deceive others by putting on an act to make themselves seem more qualified or capable than they really are. They are a smooth talker but a bluffer.

ℬ - Long beak ⸌ℬ shows putting themselves into other people's business and being nosey. Since it points to the past it shows they have something in their own past to resolve but they get involved with other people's business instead.

ℬ - A curved stem shows this person has no firm backbone. That shows they don't stay firm in beliefs or in plans. Also this stem is not touched by the rest of the letter. That shows they keep some emotional distance from others and have a hard time feeling attached.

B - Simple capitals with no fancy extras shows an intelligent person who is straight forward with nothing extra in mind except getting straight to work.

$$c \quad c$$

c is a body zone circle letter →C← like the letters a and o. Body circles show if the person is fully honest about what's on their mind or has something hidden in their mind when they have conversations with others.

C - Clear circle shows they are honest and have nothing to hide. They feel free to express themselves.

C - Line at the start of c shows there's something they are hiding in their mind. It's called evasive or sneaky because they don't tell the whole truth.

C - Beginning loop shows they are holding onto a hurt feeling from their past.

C - Snail curl shows they are most interested in talking about themselves.

C - Beginning sharp-&-short angle, called a temper tic, shows they can be quick to anger.

C - Almost closed circle shows shyness and they dislike social involvement.

(- Narrow shows they are shy, careful, won't take risks, and are not a giver or a spender. They won't want to talk much and will hold back their thoughts.

C - Bottom ends abruptly C⌐ and is shorter than the top shows they are abrupt in ending conversations.

⌣ - Bottom extends in a smile-like curve shows they are generous and extend themselves to others.

⊂ - Bottom stays flat along the baseline shows they are cautious and stay where they feel safe.

C - Round and full shows they are genuinely friendly. They like talking with others.

C - Wide shows they are broad minded, tolerant, gullible, generous, and spends money easily. They are willing to talk about anything and everything.

ᶞ ᒎ

d shows how a person evaluates their behavior.

The circle →d shows how they want others to evaluate them.

The stem d↖ shows how they evaluate their own behavior.

Circle evaluation from others:

𝑑 𝖽 - Large circle shows they want to get a lot of attention and applause from others. Lots of attention makes them feel highly evaluated by others.

𝟤 𝖽 - Small circle shows they want others pleased with the work they do without interfering. Being trusted to work alone makes them feel well evaluated by others.

𝑙 𝖽 - Narrow circle shows they want others to be impressed that they don't ask anything from them.
It makes them feel self-sufficient.

𝑑 𝖼𝗅 - Wide circle shows they need a lot of support and appreciation from others to feel well evaluated.

Stem evaluation of themselves:
(These meanings are also shown in t stems).

𝑑 𝖽 - Short head d, called independent-d, shows their self evaluation focuses on how well they feel they accomplish the list of expectations they have for themselves. They evaluate themselves independently, not from approval or praise from others.

𝟤 𝖽 - Tall head d, called pride-d, shows their self evaluation is based on the pride they feel in how well they accomplish their own tall list of expectations. The pride they feel comes from their own evaluation but they also have the need for a tall amount of approval and praise from others.

12

ℓ d - Extra tall head d (stem is at least 3x taller than the circle), called vanity-d or great-me-d, shows they base their self evaluation on their made-up belief that they are greater than others. Really they feel inferior but they over-compensate by convincing themselves they are greater. They need constant approval and praise from others to keep feeling convinced.

d - Retraced loop, called dignity-d, shows they have a very narrow view of behavior they consider proper. They evaluate themselves according to that narrow set of acceptable rules. They evaluate others that way as well, which makes them easily judgmental.

d - Moderate-width loop shows they feel a few choices of behaviors are acceptable. Their self evaluation is based on staying within those choices. If the loop is clear and smoothly written, their self evaluation is good and they are comfortable with their behavior.

ₐ - Wide loop shows they consider a wide variety of behaviors acceptable. But wide loop d, called sensitive-d, also considers a wide variety of self criticisms. They use their self criticisms to evaluate themselves. They generally evaluate themselves much harsher than they deserve.

Q - Extra wide loop, wider than the circle, is an even more sensitive-d. It shows they never stop feeling criticized. They hear any advice as criticism. They become defensive and avoid situations of criticism as much as possible. Their evaluation of themselves is a constant long list of criticisms.

∂ - d stem curved to the left, called literary-d, shows a love of literature and culture. They base their self evaluation on literary or cultural accomplishments.

$\partial\ell$ - This loop is written towards the right instead of to the left. Writing the loop towards the right shows this person does not evaluate themselves and has a hard time considering that their behavior could be wrong. Any behavior issues about them that are brought to their attention are blamed on others.

α - This d stem is separated into a tent $\wedge$ shape. The tent shape $\wedge$ is a self-protective barrier against what others say. The first tent stroke / shows protecting themselves from past criticism. The second tent stroke \ shows protecting themselves from future criticism. A tent shape in any letter shows the person is stubborn. They refuse to listen to suggestions from others due to fear of criticism. They blame any wrong behavior on others. They insist they are right and won't discuss the possibility that they are wrong. Their self evaluation is diverted to anger at the behavior of others instead of evaluating their own behavior.

Capitals show how confident they are with themselves:

D - Simple, clear capitals, with no fancy extras, show the person is confident and straight forward.

D - Oversized capitals show a large ego that wants to appear bigger and more important than they really feel inside. They like proving how big they are by being the leader. Being in charge makes them feel other people's confidence in them, which makes them feel well evaluated and confident in themselves.

D - Small size capitals show they are timid and a follower. They are not confident with others but can be confident with work they do alone.

D - Wide shows they are self-centered and want a lot of attention. They are fascinated with themselves and their own accomplishments. They need praise and attention to keep feeling confident.

D - Narrow shows they are shy, careful, fearful, and won't take chances. They feel confident when they stick to what they do well.

V - Angular shows they are self righteous, critical, defensive, and hold fast to what they want. They feel confident when they get what they demand.

D - Written as two separate parts that don't touch shows standing alone and having difficulty adjusting to others. They feel most confident left alone to do tasks their own way.

$$\mathcal{e} \; e$$

e shows how a person listens.

The shape of e← even looks like an ear.

e - Big loop in the e is called open-e. Their ears are wide open to listen to what others say. They are broad minded and don't question what is said.

e - Extra big open-e loop is extra broad-minded. They listen to and accept as okay things that are not acceptable to many others. They are extra tolerant and also extra nosey about other people.

e - Pinched closed e loops show ears closed to what others have to say. If some e loops are pinched it shows they sometimes don't want to listen. If most of their e loops are pinched, they are narrow-minded and change is very difficult for them.

e -Short end stroke e✓ shows they are abrupt. They will only listen for a short time and abruptly end conversations.

e - Long curved end stroke shows reaching out to others. They are sociable, generous, and considerate. They listen as a way to be sociable and considerate.

Ɛ - Greek e shows they are creative with words and have an appreciation of culture. They especially enjoy listening to musical and dramatic performances.

E - Firm, straight stem ⦶E (also called firm, straight backbone) shows they stick firm to their beliefs and won't bend their beliefs to please others.

Ɛ - Curved backbone shows they bend to other people's beliefs. They are easily influenced by what they hear from others and easily bend their beliefs to please them.

Capital E arms and leg represent the 3 zones:

E - Top arm represents the head thinking zone. Top arm that is longer than the others shows they rely on their intellectual strengths.

E - Top arm that is shorter than the others shows they have a hard time understanding intellectual ideas and also have a hard time understanding what might be expected of them from others.

Ɛ - Middle arm represents the body social interaction zone. Middle arm that is longer than the others shows they tend to intrude on other people socially.

E - Middle arm that is shorter than the others shows they respect other people's space.

E - Bottom leg represents the leg physical action zone. Bottom leg that is longer than the arms shows they feel energetic and physically strong.

E - Bottom leg that is shorter than the arms shows they feel physically inadequate.

$$ƒ f$$

ƒ f - shows the person's strengths when it comes to organizing ideas into practical plans & action.

ƒ f - Tall head ƒ or high crossbar f show they are strong in coming up with lofty theoretical or idealistic ideas for their plans.

ƒ f - Moderately-tall head ƒ or crossbar in the middle f show they are strong in coming up with practical ideas for their plans.

ƒ f - Short head ƒ or low crossbar f show they are best at coming up with short-term ideas that are easy to do.

ƒ f - Long lower loop ƒ or long crossbar f show they are strong on doing the physical action work for as long as it takes to make their plan happen.

_f_ f - Moderate length lower loop _f_ or moderate length crossbar f show they are strong on doing a moderate and practical amount of the physical work to make their plan happen.

_f_ f - Short bottom loop _f_ or short crossbar f show they are not strong at doing the physical work to make their plan happen. They may do a little, but get bored and give up quickly.

_f_ f - Top & bottom halves both at least moderate-length, plus on print f at least a moderate length crossbar, show the person is strong in both thinking of an idea and doing the physical work to make their plan happen.

_f_ _f_ - Short top loop or low cross-bar, show they don't have their own ideas but may be willing to do the physical work for someone else's idea.

_f_ - This extra middle loop _f_ is called a persistence-loop.

It shows the person has a strong emotional purpose that pushes them to keep working to make their plan happen. They believe that if at first they don't succeed, try try again. And they do keep trying until they find a way to make it work.

ƒ f - No top loop ᴈƒ or no full hook ƒᴿ show their
ideas are already set and they don't require any more
thought to proceed directly into the physical action.

ƒ f - Fluid and graceful shows their speaking is
naturally fluid and graceful. They can easily explain
their plans and organize the physical work for it
gracefully. They enjoy the arts and would be natural
at arranging art events.

Capital F shows a person's ability for learning and plans
for their future:

 F - Short top arm shows they are unable to see facts
clearly and may not be able to learn what they need for
their future.

F - Long second arm shows they are more interested
in socializing than learning what they need to know to
succeed in their future.

F - Longer top arm with straight backbone shows they
have the learning ability and the firm backbone to be
successful in their future.

F F - Curved backbone shows they bend to what
others want and don't have firm beliefs they stick
to. They also bend to doing other activities instead of
sticking firm to what they need to do for their future.

𝓕 - Wavy arms show they have a sense of humor they like to use. Their humor keeps people around them smiling and happy to help get their things done.

𝒴𝓕 - Top arm with a big hook shows they like to collect things. Their future would be suited to a position where there are things to collect.

> 𝑔 𝟫 ◄

𝑔 is for go-getter. The leg physical-action zone in 𝟫◄ is a great place to see: Do they go-get with gusto or go-get while grumbling? (Also see y section. The 'will-try list' meanings of y legs also apply to g legs.)

𝒴 𝟫 - Narrow-short legs (narrower and shorter than the body circle) show they go-get while grumbling. They don't expect to enjoy new activities and they don't expect much from themselves or others.

𝑔 𝟫 - Moderate width & length legs (legs longer and narrower than circle) show they enjoy physical activities. They go-get with gusto, do a lot, and enjoy the feeling of accomplishment.

g g - Wide legs (as wide as the body circle) show they are interested in a wide variety of activities and have very wide range of expectations to achieve. They go-get with gusto, always having a lot they want to do.

g g - Extra wide legs (wider than the body circle) show they always imagine they should be doing more than they can possibly do. No matter how much they actually do, they feel they should do and achieve more. Wide round g loops *g* are sometimes called money bags because what some people want to achieve is material wealth. Whatever this person wants to achieve, whether it's their personal goals or wealth, they go-get with gusto. They always want to do more.

g g - Short legs show they get bored quickly. Their go-getting only lasts a short time and they give up fast. If pushed to do more, they go-get while grumbling.

g g - moderately-long legs (longer than circle) show they can stick to tasks to get them done. They will go-get with gusto for a while, but unless it's of high interest to them, after a moderate amount of time they start to lose their excitement.

g g - Long legs (2-3 times as long as circle) show they have determination that sticks to their go-getting for a very long time and accomplishes a lot. They are task oriented and always doing something. They also don't like having to stop.

g - Extra long legs (more than 3 times as long as circle) show they have so much go-getting in them they are constantly restless. What calms them down is being involved in physically doing something or else thinking about go-getting to somewhere else. They're always ready to change their décor or location.

q - Legs that are a straight down line show they want to do their go-getting alone.

g - Legs pulled to the left show they long to go-get back to their past for the love and support they feel they missed out on.

g - Legs pushed to the right show they are pushing all their social energy into their work. They feel more satisfaction to go-get with gusto in their work than they do in their social life.

g - Angles in legs show they have some past angry feeling that makes them demanding. Their go-getting makes demands on others.

g - Legs that arc to the left often show they are trying to cover up feelings of guilt. Their guilt is the feeling that they were responsible for something bad that happened. They keep it hidden though they really may not be responsible for what happened at all. They go-get grudgingly into anything with responsibility because they feel too guilt-ridden to be trusted.

g/g - A tiny circle at the bottom of the legs show they are clannish. That means they hold tightly to only a few carefully selected people and don't want anyone else getting close to them. Their go-getting goes into controlling their few selected people. They want total loyalty and don't want them go-getting anywhere with anyone else.

8 g - Figure-8 g that's written gracefully, shows they are financially and socially resourceful. They like go-getting with money and in style.

q - g legs that curve to the right like a q(Q) show their legs moving away from themselves to help others. They are altruistic and like doing their go-getting for others.

G G - Capitals plain and simple show they are intelligent and straight forward. They go-get without delay.

G - Squared shows they are practical and good at constructing with their hands. They go-get with exact plans of what to construct or do.

G - Sharp downstrokes show they are critical. They go-get while sharply criticizing others.

G - Large and very rounded shows they seek affection. They go-get with friendliness.

G - Large and open on top shows they need lots of mental and physical things to do. They go-get with gusto, always open to more things to do.

G - Small and very narrow shows they are slow to act and react. They don't like moving forward from where they currently are and go-get while grumbling.

h h

h is an easy letter to see if a person's talents are used or held back.

The stem to the head $\nearrow h$ gets the idea for using their talent.

Use of the talent is in the thinking space between the stem & hump: h (has space) - h (has no space)

Making the plan to use the talent is in the hump h←.

Stem to the head $\nearrow h$:

h h- Tall stem shows they prefer idealistic or theoretical ideas for their talents. They want to change the world or bring the world a new idea.

_h_ h - Moderate height heads show they prefer practical ideas that have a way to use their talents to improve themselves, their school, their work or their community.

_h_ h - Short heads show they prefer ideas that involve using their talents to improve their own situation at home, school or work.

Thinking space between the stem & hump h-or-h shows if their talent is used:

Thinking space that's open to the baseline like these →h→h, shows the talent is being used.

Some thinking space that's partly open to the baseline like these →h→h, shows some talent is being used.

No thinking space like these →h→h, shows their talent is being held back.

Making the plan to use the talent is in the hump h←:

h - Narrow hump shows there is inner doubt holding them back from moving forward with a plan for their talent.

h - Moderate width hump shows good confidence to make a plan for their talent.

h - Wide hump shows they need emotional support from others to give them confidence to make a plan for their talent.

h h - Angled hump shows they make quick decisions and go right into action for their talent.

h h - Curved hump shows they take time to consider lots of possible different plans before they take action.

h h - Hump leg stops short shows they hold back committing to their plan.

H H - Persistence-loop →H shows the person keeps trying till they find a plan that works. They don't give up.

H H - Rising-up crossbar shows they are optimistic and ambitious. They want to prove how much they can do and that they can do it better than others. That is their motivation to use their talent.

H H - High crossbar shows they think highly of themselves. They feel above and superior to others. This makes them more interested in themselves than making a solid practical plan to put their talent to use.

Ĥ H - Low crossbar shows they stay close to what's practical for them day to day. This makes them only pursue a plan that is a sure thing. They don't want any risks.

H Ĥ - Heavy crossbar H shows strong energy while extra-long crossbar Ĥ shows willful, meaning they will impose their plan on others if others get in the way. Heavy & long crossbars push right through obstacles. Both show they have a strong inner drive and will strongly challenge anything that tries to stop them.

Ĥ H - Light crossbar shows they have weak energy for pushing forward with their plan. They also have a yielding nature that easily gives in to what other people want them to do. They have very little drive to pursue their plan.

H Ĥ - Convex ⌒ crossbar shows they keep strong self control of their feelings. They feel they have to keep their real feelings hidden. They work best alone if they decide to pursue a plan.

Ĥ H - Concave ⌣ crossbar shows they are easily led, and not strongly committed to their own plan. They may have fun talking about it but not the strong drive to see it through.

28

Ii & Jj

i & j are the only letters with a dot on top. The dot shows where the person's attention naturally goes.

i j - Dots placed very close to the stem ↗i j↖ show the person's attention stays very close to their task. They pay very close attention to details.

l J - No dots show the person doesn't pay attention to the details. Their attention is either on getting done fast or else they are careless.

ı ʋ - high dots show their attention is on ideas more than details. The higher the dot the more imagination they are using.

ⁱ j̄ - Dots pushed into a line show the person is irritated. Their attention is on what's bothering them.

i j - Heavy dots show they are strong willed and materialistic. Their attention is on how to get their desired possessions, living comforts, and fine food.

i j - Light dots show they are timid, unassertive, and sensitive. Their attention is on what might hurt them and avoiding it.

i ⟩ - Circle dots show the person likes to be seen as creative and unique. Their attention is on getting others to notice how creative and unique they are.

♡ ♡ - Heart dots show the person likes thinking of love. Their attention is on finding love and romance.

Capital I shows how a person sees themselves:

I - Extra large I shows they have an exaggerated sense of their self importance. They see themselves as more important than others.

IABC - Capital I that is taller than their other capitals shows they have a big ego but lack real self confidence. They see themselves as larger than others and feel they should get more attention than others get.

IABC - I that is the same size as their other capitals shows they have good self confidence. They see themselves as capable to do what they want and they don't need any special attention.

I - Long support crossbars on top and bottom ↗I↙ show they need ongoing emotional or financial support from their parents or others who support them.

I - A simple line for I shows they feel independent in their abilities without need of support.

ᵒ *j̇ j* ᵒ

j legs, like legs in g-p-q-y, show how a person handles their follow through physical action.

j̇ j - Short legs show they have short follow through action. They get bored quickly and give up fast.

j̇ j - Long legs show they have long follow through action. Long legs are called determination. They stick with their 'active doing' for as long as it takes. Active doing can be any physical action or sitting activity. No matter what they're doing, they are doing something. A long legs person is a 'doer.'

j̇ j - Straight line leg shows their follow through action follows a straight path. They don't like detours, changes, or interruptions.

j̇ j - Curved leg shows their follow through action is flexible to try other possibilities. They take more time but if the leg is long they stick with it to get it done.

j̇ j - Legs that curve left on the bottom ‿ show the person takes time to think before they act on their follow through action.

$\bar{r} \ j$ - Legs that push straight forward to the right ↗ are called aggressive. That shows the person is too excited or too angry to take time to think. They just push ahead and don't let anything stop them in their follow through action.

$\dot{v}$ - If the push forward line is straight and heavy, it shows they can get physically aggressive and also shows they can easily get angry. If the anger is very strong they might physically push someone out of their way to do their follow through action.

$g J$ - Clear and simple capitals with top & bottom fairly balanced in size, show they are overall confident, capable, and independent. They are ready for follow through action.

$\gamma \ J$ - No upper loop or crossbar show their decisions are already set and they want to get started on their follow through action without delay.

$7]$ - Partial upper loop or crossbar on left only, show they block out other people's input. They make decisions by themselves for their follow through action.

$\int U$ - Narrow upper loop or crossbar show they are inhibited, shy, and hesitant to take chances. They hesitate before moving into follow through action.

J- Wide upper loop or crossbar show they have a lot of ideas in mind for future follow up action.

J - Narrow lower loop or narrow hook show they hold back on their follow through action.

J - Very wide lower loop or very wide hook show they like fantasizing a lot about different possible follow through actions.

J - Sharp angled lower loop or hook show they are impatient and insistent with others in their follow through actions.

J - Straight stem *J*← *J*← shows they have a firm backbone, meaning they are firm in their beliefs and firm in standing up for themselves. They also stand firm in what they want their follow through action to be.

J - Curved stem *J*← *J*← shows they have a bending backbone that doesn't always stand up for themselves and their beliefs. They sometimes bend their ideas to what others believe and sometimes bend their follow through action to what others want done.

𝒌 k

k shows how a person deals with authority.

The backbone (also called stem) →k shows how a person stands up for themselves against authority.

The arm k↖ shows how a person reacts to authority.

The leg k↙ shows how that authority is accepted and put to practical use.

𝒌 k - Straight backbone shows the person is able to stand up to authority when they don't agree with what they're told.

ƙ k - Curved backbone shows the person caves-in to authority rather than stands up to it.

𝒌 k - All 3 of backbone-arm-leg in balanced proportion, shows the person accepts the authority of those in charge if they think it's reasonable for the situation.

ƙ ƙ - Arm that pushes up taller than x-height shows quick defiance. They are quick to defy authority and accuse others of being wrong or unfair.

k h - Arm stays shorter than leg shows the person is humble in the face of authority. They accept authority even when they don't agree.

k k - Leg stops high above baseline shows the person won't act on orders from authority. They get impatient and irritable when an authority tells them what to do.

k k - Leg that pushes below baseline shows the person is defensive and self protective against authority. They insist their own decisions and actions are right.

k k - Leg is a rounded hump shows the person needs lots of time to consider various possible reactions to authority. Their reactions are kept inside until they decide how to react.

k k - Arm and leg that smoothly avoid touching the backbone show the person handles authority by smoothly handling the issue. They remain objective and avoid confronting or defying authority directly.

k k - Straight lines that touch the backbone in a sharp angle show a quick understanding of what the authority wants and a quick reaction to resolve it right then and there. They get impatient with a delay.

$\mathcal{K}$ - Sharp angle pulled back over the backbone shows the person is holding onto anger at being judged by others in their past. This anger gets added to anger at being judged by authority in the present.

$\mathcal{K}$- Arm and leg pulled over backbone in a curve show they are concerned how authorities from their past would judge them in the present. The curve shows they still want to please their past authorities.

k - A curve touching the backbone shows a quick smooth handling of authority while being friendly with a smile. They generally avoid confrontation and get free of any restrictions on them as gently as possible.

$\mathcal{K}$ - Loop around the backbone shows their feelings to others, including authority, is with affection. They want to please and will easily offer a hug.

$\mathcal{K}$ - Loop on the left side of stem shows they strongly feel the loss of a special relationship. The emotions in the loop come up often, including when they need to stand up for themselves.

ℓl

l is for learning & ideas they will consider. As the only letter that goes straight to the head without a body circle or hump, it's free to only show a person's ability to learn ideas and how they use them.

ℓl - Tall ℓ shows the person finds it easy to learn new ideas and spends lots of time thinking about them. They think idealistically and theoretically, meaning what is ideal or best for the world beyond what exists or is factually proven. They could consider topics such as global social issues, spiritual faith, or theories about the universe.

ℓl - Moderately-tall ℓ shows the person has an easy time learning new ideas but is only really interested in ideas that can have a practical purpose. They consider topics that are practical for where they live and what they can realistically do. Ideas about improving their environment or helping those in need are of interest if they can be realistic for them to do.

ℓl - Short ℓ shows this person finds it difficult to learn new ideas. They don't see the point in ideas that are not immediately practical and consider anything else a waste of time. They could consider ideas with a specific practical use, such as improving their home, job, or helping others in their family or community with practical tasks.

ℓℚ - Wide loop shows the person is interested in a wide range of ideas and considers them all. Their broad-minded outlook gives them an anything goes philosophy, a permissive attitude, and a tendency to bend the rules. Their wide loop also shows a very active imagination. Their thinking is creative and always changing with their new ideas. They have a hard time sticking to a decision because their mind is always active, either considering something new or going over and over the same ideas considering new ways to see them.

ℓ ℓ - Moderate width loop shows this person considers a moderate variety of ideas that are reasonable for the situation. They keep a flexible attitude, make reasonable decisions, then stick to them for as long as it seems the right way to proceed. Their adaptable attitude works well with others and keeps a flexible open mind that will change their decision when presented with good reasons.

l *ℓ* - Narrow loop shows this person sticks with a narrow range of ideas and is not interested in new ways to see their ideas. Their narrow-minded outlook makes them opinionated, meaning they think that only one idea is the right one. They don't see the point in considering anything else, unless there's a very important reason.

all *all* -In double *ℓℓ* *ll* words if the first *ℓ* is much taller it shows that person feels intellectually superior.
They can be arrogant or snobbish.

all *all* - In double *ℓℓ* *ll* words if the first *ℓ* is a little taller, they are diplomatic. They notice when others feel low and want to raise their feelings up. If they notice the other person feels less smart or less important, they want to make the other person feel their thoughts are smart or important, too.

all *all* -In double *ℓℓ* *ll* words if the first one is shorter it shows that person feels others are intellectually superior. They feel looked down on and self conscious. They fear ridicule from others and that others will pounce on their mistakes.

$\mathcal{L}$ L - Clear and simple capitals show they are intelligent, capable and have a direct manner. They are ready to work, they don't need anything extra from anyone and don't want to waste their time on unnecessary chit chat.

L - Right angled shape shows they are free thinking, have a sharp mind, and get impatient if they can't get directly to work. They also like to build things. They make precise plans and stick to them.

$\mathcal{L}$ - Large top loops $\mathcal{L}$ show the person feels it's important to be generous and to take care of others. They believe it's the right thing to do.

$\mathcal{L}$ - Large baseline loop $\mathcal{L}$ shows they are strongly self motivated. They also have strong practical sense, good common sense with money, and often have a good fashion sense as well.

$\mathcal{L}$ - Small baseline loop $\mathcal{L}$ shows they have a gentle nature that's motivated by feelings of proving their abilities to themselves. These self motivated feelings help them stick to their goals.

$\mathcal{L}$ - Humped bottom $\mathcal{L}$ shows the person keeps their thinking to themselves. They consider their thoughts private and don't like others prying into their business.

m n

m and n show a person's thinking style.

Angles *M N* show exploratory & analytical thinking.

Curvy humps m n show imaginative & creative thinking.

Needle points *m M* show lightning fast thinking.

People think with all the styles you see in their writing.

mn MN - Angles V or Λ in letters m or n show a person's thinking is sharp and quick. Angles formed by straight lines show they follow a straight logical plan and move straight forward to put it into action.

mn MN - Angles that point up sharply ↑Λ show the person has strong curiosity and a probing mind that explores for new information. They research beyond simple explanations to figure out new explanations for why something is the way it is.

mn MN - Angles that point down sharply ↓V show the person is a sharp analyzer. They focus right in on the facts of a problem, quickly get to the point of what's important and what it means, then figure out a precise solution.

mⁿ mn - Curved humps Ω show thinking that slowly and carefully mulls over information for a long while. This person learns by repeating information over and over until they understand it fully. The hump is closed on top which shows their thinking is kept to themselves and they don't want input from others. The curve in the hump shows they add imagination and feelings to their thinking. They take a lot of time but their conclusions are often creative and original.

M N - Humps with a beginning V like →M→N show an easy time getting to the point of information.

m n - Humps without a beginning V like→m→n show a hard time getting to the point of information.

μ M - Needle points up M show the person thinks very fast and makes instant decisions. They have a sharp mind and know a lot.

〜〜〜 - Wavy with all curves that looks like a piece of thread is called thready. If this is their writing for others to read it shows their thinking has no firm beliefs or ideas. They go with the flow of what's easiest at the moment. Their thinking is about how to get what they want with the least effort. They take the path of least resistance and avoid responsibility or commitment. If the person is writing extra fast and it's just for them to read, then thready looking can simply mean their thinking is faster than their hand.

m M - Cursive m has 3 humps. First hump represents the 'me'. Second hump represents the 'you' the person is thinking about. The third hump represents the 'they' which can mean their family or a group in their society. The tallest hump shows whose approval is most important to the person - me, you, or they. The shortest hump shows whose approval is least important to the person. When they are all equal height, they are all equally important.

m M - When doing their thinking, this person puts approval by 'me' first, approval by 'you' second, and approval by 'they' third.

m m - When doing their thinking, this person puts approval by 'me' first, approval by 'they' second, and approval by 'you' third.

M - When doing their thinking, this person puts approval by 'you' first.

M - When doing their thinking, this person puts approval by 'they' first. This is called being self conscious. They feel looked down on by others and fear they will be ridiculed.

m M - Print m has 2 humps. With only two humps the first hump refers to 'me', the second hump refers to 'you'.

m ᴍ - First hump taller is a 'me to you' situation called diplomatic. This person (me) feels their own high status of ability, notices when the other person feels lower than them, and they want to raise the other person's feelings so they don't feel uncomfortably lower.

ʍ M - Second hump taller is a 'me to you' situation called self conscious. This person (me) feels a lower level of ability compared to the 'you' and feels the 'you' is looking down on them. They fear they will be ridiculed.

ᴍᴍ - Loops under humps are called worry loops. They anticipate problems beyond what's practical and cautious. They spend a lot of time and energy on worrying. If they have a lot of worry loops, their general feeling of worry fills them with a continual sense of distress.

m M - When the middle stroke doesn't reach the baseline it shows the person gives a short effort to their thinking. They don't feel the need to spend time thinking deeply. Quick solutions suit them best.

M ᴍ - When the first stroke doesn't reach the baseline it shows the person feels insecure about making a decision.

m n - When the last stroke doesn't reach the baseline it shows the person ends their thinking abruptly before coming to a final decision. It also shows they tend to end relationships suddenly.

M N - Caved-in right side shows the person feels insecure and pressured by the future. They fear they won't be able to manage what they need to do and cave-in to their fear instead of forging ahead. They avoid making decisions.

M N - Caved-in lines that come to a sharp point are called sharks teeth. The caved-in lines forming a sharp point show they feel pressured into a corner. The sharp point also shows the person feels some anger. They are on a very strong alert to protect themselves. They will talk their way out of a situation if they can. If there are several sharks teeth in the writing they could feel the urge to strike out first before they are attacked.

mn mn - Last stroke curls in or out shows the person is wound up in themselves. They are mainly self absorbed. Their thinking is about manipulating to get what they want.

mn MN - Square shaped letters show the person thinks with mechanical precision. They have mechanical skill and constructive ability.

𝓂 𝓃 - Long and wavy lead-ins show they have a big sense of humor. Their light hearted remarks add to their charm and relieve tension in a room.

𝓂 𝓃 - Smile curve lead-ins show they put on a smiley face and are thoughtful of others. The angle where this smile curve meets this stem 𝓂 shows there are angry feelings covered up by this smile.

𝓂 𝓃 - Straight lead-ins at a square angle show a sharp wit. Notice that this sharp angle 𝓂 points to their past. That shows they feel some sharp resentment towards their past which gives them the tendency for sharp remarks.

𝓂𝓂 - Short sharp angled lead-ins are called temper tics. They show a quick temper where the person can get angry fast.

𝓂 𝓃 - Hump lead-ins show carefulness. They are careful and cautious in what they do or say.

𝓃 𝓃 - Hook lead-ins show the person is possessive. They cling possessively to either people, physical objects, or the goals they want to achieve.

𝓂 𝓂 - Bottom hooks or curls on both sides are called money claws. They show the person tends to be greedy and wants to possess a lot of money or material objects.

Mm- Starting big loop shows the person wants a chance to prove they can handle responsibility. They are willing to take on more work to prove it.

m n m m n - Upper left lead-ins that are tight small loops *m*, or flattened loops *n*, or point to the upper left *m m n*, all indicate jealousy. The person feels someone else received the love that should have come to them and they still feel the fear that they are not loved. Some people cover their jealousy with a smile *m*. Many people use their jealousy as a motivator to prove how great they are to themselves and others. Jealousy is common, often turning family or friends into competitors. It's up to the person how they use those feelings. Being aware of the feelings makes it easier to use them as positive motivation and not continue to feel bad.

M n - Ending stroke pushed down into the action zone shows they have adamantly put their foot down to illustrate their insistent action. They won't compromise and won't change their mind. They don't really feel confident but insist on their way to prove to themselves and others that their decisions are right. They may step on others if necessary to get what they insist on.

M M - Sharp points with a curved middle show a person who bends away from traditional ways of thinking. They

47

constantly search for new easy answers and are easily influenced by fads in health, diet, and appearance.

ᴍ M -Two humps connected by a middle curve is called a double-bow. It is all curves which shows the person is indecisive, avoids conflict, and wants to please others. They also change their opinions and beliefs depending on who they are with. They will happily stick to daily routines and manual tasks since it pleases others and they don't have to make any decisions.

ơ O

o is a body zone circle letter. Like a & c, o shows what's on a person's mind when they talk to others.

ơ O - Circle that's clear inside shows the person is straight forward with nothing to hide. Also a nicely rounded circle shows the person is nice to others.

ℓ 0 - Narrow shows the person has self doubts about their abilities. They are introverted and are most comfortable keeping to themselves. They do feel comfortable talking about things they actually do and know well.

Ⅱ - Very narrow shows they are tense and rigid about rules or what's acceptable. They tend not to talk about feelings and have trouble accepting compliments about themselves. They feel only actual actions should be talked about.

◯ ◯ - Wide shows they need many compliments and emotional support from others. They need many people to keep telling them how good they are at what they do. They also like to talk about themselves.

𝜎 0 - Closed at top shows they keep their thoughts to themselves. They only speak when they feel it's important or necessary.

𝜎0 - Knotted at top shows they tied themselves off from talking to most others, except to the few they trust. They may appear cold, distant, and inclined toward secrecy, but it's really more that they believe in giving information on a need-to-know basis.

(9 U - Open top shows the person is talkative, sociable, and shares easily. The bigger the opening, the more they like to talk.

(6 ◌ - Hooks and lines inside the circles show hidden plans in the person's mind. They keep these plans to themselves and don't want to reveal them to others. A curved line like a smile ◌ shows they protect their hidden plans with a smile. A straight line that comes to a sharp point ◌ is called a stinger. It shows they protect those plans with a nasty sharp tongue. Long inside lines ◌ are called back stabbers. They probably won't actually stab a person in the back but they talk

friendly while they plan something hurtful which can be called a stab in the back. They all keep their real plans hidden and manipulate to get what they want.

O↖ O↖ - Loop that ends on the right is called secrecy. It shows the person keeps personal feelings and secrets from others. The size of the loop shows the size of the space the personal feelings or secrets take up in the person's mind. The bigger the loop the bigger the person's fear that someone will get hurt or they will be ridiculed if they tell others their hidden thoughts.

↗O ↗O - Loop that begins on the left is called denial. It shows the person is not ready to face the truth about what they are doing or feeling.

⊖ - Loops on both sides that overlap each other show their thinking is confused by both secrets and denial of the truth. They feel they have to protect all the various private thoughts they are hiding. To protect these thoughts they will tell part of the truth but not the whole truth. Sometimes the confusion of all they're hiding makes it easier for them to lie.

◎ - Extra lines around a circle show the person feels the need to build a stronger wall around them. They feel the need to be self protective and are difficult to get to know. They keep a poker face, don't show their feelings, and won't talk about what's on their mind for fear of embarrassment.

♡ ♥ - Heart shape for an o shows the person longs for love and romance. They like talking about love, romance, and feelings.

𝒬 𝒬 - Final line in o that returns to baseline like an 'a' shows the person feels insecure and needs the security of touching their baseline. Touching the baseline when it's not necessary for the letter, shows they need the feeling of home-based comfort and security they get from being where it's familiar and comfortable for them. They also like talking about what's familiar and comfortable for them.

𝓅 𝓟

p is the only letter to show how strong or vulnerable a person feels physically before showing how strong or vulnerable they feel emotionally in relationships. That is because p is the only letter with the leg before the body-circle.

↘p leg shows how strong or vulnerable a person feels physically.

p← circle shows how strong or vulnerable a person feels in relationships.

↗ᑭ stem that goes above the circle into the head zone shows a person feels their strongest when defending ideas.

⤵p leg shows how strong or vulnerable a person feels physically:

ℓ ℓ - Light pressure legs (or light pressure whole letters) show they feel physically weak and vulnerable. They enjoy light physical activity but they have a low supply of energy. Strenuous activity makes them feel tired and more vulnerable. They can make strong attachments and commitments to others but they often don't show the strong feelings they have because they are conserving energy. They also conserve their energy by taking in strong feelings a little at a time and then showing them a little at a time.

ρ ρ - Heavy pressure legs (or whole letters) show they feel strong and have strong long lasting energy. They want a lot of physical activity and physical activity makes them feel stronger. They make strong attachments and long-term commitments to others. Their feelings are deeply felt, deeply held, strongly shown, and rarely change.

ℓ p - Short legs show they feel weak with low energy. They only commit to short times with others. They want relationships with little effort that don't require a lot of work. They easily feel vulnerable and threatened by others. They feel safest at home.

p p - Moderate length p to long p, with moderate to heavy pressure, show they feel physically strong and have good energy. They willingly commit their time to others and are willing to work for a long lasting relationship. They like working with others to get things done. The more they accomplish the stronger they feel.

p - Extra long leg with moderate pressure shows they need a lot of physical activity, have long lasting energy, but only feel strong when they're physically active. When they're not active they feel vulnerable and restless. To stop feeling vulnerable they must be active and constantly doing. When not active they daydream about going somewhere else or a new project to do like changing something in their home. Extra long legs is called desire for change.

p p - Leg loop that's retraced over itself shows the person feels the need to double up their defenses against feeling vulnerable. They close themselves off from others to feel less vulnerable and stronger. With the retraced descender they feel good physical strength to protect themselves. They're most interested in physical activity they can do alone and that has precise purposeful moves. Mastering those precise moves makes them feel strong.

ρ ρ - Narrow leg loop shows they feel vulnerable and hesitant to try unfamiliar physical activities. They prefer taking action alone or with only a few others.

ℓ ℓ - Moderate width loop with moderate pressure shows the person feels strong and is interested in trying a variety of activities. They have strong endurance and enjoy physical exercise. They enjoy group activities and can commit to relationships with others.

ℓ ℓ - Wide leg loops show the person needs a lot of physical activity and is physically restless. They also want their physical actions noticed and may tend to show off. Their wide loops also hold imagination and feelings that can make them feel vulnerable. But doing a lot and getting a lot of attention from others makes them feel confident and stronger.

ρ ρ - Angle at bottom of leg that pushes up & forward ↗ shows they feel strong. They have energy they want to put to work immediately. In relationships they will commit but can easily get impatient. When they feel threatened, they can get aggressive.

p← circle shows how strong or vulnerable a person feels in relationships:

℘ P - Circles that are moderate ℘ to P large sized show they feel strong enough in relationships to feel worthy of love from others and take the risk of loving them back.

ᵖ ρ - Small circles show they feel emotionally vulnerable and are hesitant to enter a loving relationship with others.

ᵧ ℿ - Soft tops and open bottoms show they feel vulnerable in relationships. They are easily accepting and swayed by what others want. They often feel too vulnerable to stand up for themselves.

ρ ℙ - Circles pushed away from their stems show they tend to feel too emotionally vulnerable to accept that others love them. But they do reach out with love for others.

P ℘ - Bubble tops show they enclose themselves in a protective bubble. They feel vulnerable with the need to protect themselves from others.

℗ ℗ -Snail curls inside the circles show they feel vulnerable that others will hurt them. They protect themselves by putting their own needs first. They are wound up in themselves and will reach out to others only if, and only for as long as, it's in their own best interests.

↗ℙ stem that goes above the circle shows a person feels their strongest when defending ideas:

ℙ - Straight stems above their circles show they feel strongest when they're debating or arguing facts, ideas, or opinions. This is called debater-p or argumentative-p. They enjoy mental challenges and are quick to get into a debate or argument.

ℙ - Stems above their circles with an angle on top is a temper tic on their argumentative-p. This person is quick to anger and always ready to argue. Arguing with others makes them feel stronger.

ℙ - Stems above their circles with a loop on top show the person goes beyond the facts in debates. They add feelings and imaginative possibilities into their opinions. They argue with emotion and feel a strong emotional need to justify or defend their idea. The added strength of using their emotions makes them feel stronger.

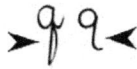

ƍ is perfect to see a person's future quest action as ૧ leg is the only descender that faces the future ૧→. A personal quest is a search or learning experience that has a personal purpose for a person's future. If a quest reaches its goal, the person gains a feeling of personal fulfillment.

↘ƒ legs show the action abilities a person has to fulfill their personal quest... or really their ability to fulfill any action they want to take.

ƍ ૧ - Long legs are called determination. Long legs show they stick with the action needed for their quest for as long as it takes, even years.

ૡ ૧ - Short legs show they only spend a short amount of time on their quest action. They give up easily and fast. This person only fulfills short & easy quests on their own. With help and encouragement they can do more.

ƍ ૧ - light pressure legs show they only have weak physical energy for their quests. Their action can be slow and steady, or else fast at times with stops to rest. They take longer but if their legs are long, they keep at it.

q q - Heavy pressure legs show they have long lasting physical energy for their quests. Their physical energy stays strong for the length of the leg. With short legs they give up after a short time. With long legs, their strong energy lasts for as long as the quest takes.

q q - Straight legs show they focus their energy to stick straight to their quest. They have a straight plan of action to reach their goal, and don't like being slowed by changes along the way.

q q - Curved legs show they stay flexible to alternate ways that would improve their quest. Their action stays open to new ideas to consider if they would better fulfill their goal, even if it takes longer.

y - Angle bottom legs show they push hard with aggressive action. They are forceful in their quest and if the line pushing up has moderate or strong pressure, they will push through difficult obstacles in their way.

Q Q - Simple and clear capitals show they will follow a practical and direct plan for their quest.

Q Q - Fancy swashes or flourishes on capitals show they are very concerned with how their quest appears to others.

Q - Heavy pressure on the tail Q shows strong energy for their personal quests.

Q Q - Wavy tails show they will be friendly and flexible to suggestions that improve their quests.

Q Q - Lines inside the circle show something in their quest involves a reason or plan they keep hidden.

Q *Q* - Snail curls show something in their quest involves manipulating others for their self interests.

2 *2* - Shows they were taught to write cursive Q like a 2 to make writing faster. This person enjoys quests that involve traditions they grew up with and pursues their quests efficiently.

r r

r reveals talents. This little letter of lines, curves, and possibly loops, shows much about the person's natural abilities.

r r - Flat top looks like a building block and shows talent for building and mechanical work with their hands. It also shows good foot coordination for dance and sports. The flat top shows a smooth line of the person's movement with no lines or loops to interfere with their movement's smooth flow.

ᴫ r - Rounded top with moderate or heavy pressure shows slow creative thinking. Their imagination considers many possibilities combined in many ways. Their talent is putting together something unique and creative.

ᴧ ᴋ - Points that point up↑ show sharp thinking. Their talent is their natural curiosity to learn more.

√ᴧ ʋ - Points that point down ↓ show strong talent for solving problems. They get to the point of the problem and find a good solution fast.

ᴙ ᴦ - Loops that point up show a talent for talking or singing. Words or songs roll smoothly off their tongue.

ᴫ r - Narrow shows they hold back showing their talents. They feel it's not proper to put themselves on display. Their talent is being humble, though quite possibly they have hidden talents they will reveal in time.

ᴙ ᴧ - When r has a side that looks like a Greek Ɛ like these ᴙ←ᴧ←, it shows their personal appearance is important to them. They have a talent for fashion and style.

R R - Simple and clear capitals show their talent is for being direct and practical. They are straight forward, intelligent, and efficient.

R R - Added dramatic flourishes show their talent is for attracting attention. They definitely enjoy getting noticed and finding ways to do it.

aRe - Capital R used instead of lowercase r shows their talent is in fashion. They are a clothes-horse and like choosing just the right clothes.

aRe - Extra large size capital R used instead of lowercase r is called a jump-up-r. This shows they sometimes suddenly behave in a surprising way. Their talent is for their sudden surprising reactions. Though their reactions are unpredictable and can be demanding. Also, since - aRe - shows they are a clothes-horse, making the capital R extra large shows they tend to like their clothing extra loose.

R R - Right side has a double curve shows they have a talent for finding the easiest and simplest solutions that please everyone. They are flexible and don't hold definite opinions they feel they must stick to.

𝓼 S

s shows common sense and the assertiveness to say Yes or No. The letter s is all body zone which is concerned only with what's practical. The way a person writes their s shows if they use their practical common sense to say an assertive Yes or No - or do they give in to what others want?

𝓼 s - Curved top shows the person is gentle, likes to please others, and always wants to say yes. Their decisions are based on their feelings of wanting to please instead of common sense. Their first reaction is a Yes. If it's not possible for them to say yes, they'll say a non-assertive, "Sorry, I really wish I could say yes."

◣ S - Straight lines show they make logical common sense decisions and are assertive. If they have some curves they add a smile to their assertive Yes or No.

◭ S - Angular shows they are strongly adamant and give a quick common sense response. Expect them to say a very assertive YES, or else a NO WAY NO HOW!

◭ S - Both straight lines & round curves show they use both logical common sense and friendly feelings in their decisions. They will give friendly smiles along with their assertive Yes or No.

ᴐ 𝒮 - Bottoms that are open *ᴐ* or short *𝒮* show they are very easily influenced by their needs and feelings. They have common sense but their needs & feelings will also influence them. Their common sense will choose Yes or No, but their feelings and needs might change their minds later on.

⊿ S - Closed or full bottoms show their common sense is closed off to their under-the-surface needs and feelings. With some straight lines their common sense is strong and they easily say an assertive Yes or No.

ℰ 𝒮 - Flowing bottom loop to write the s faster shows smart common sense thinking with a gifted flowing manner of talking. They quickly and gracefully say a Yes or No.

ℐ 𝒮 - Snail curls show their selfish feelings are stronger than their common sense. If it suits their own selfish purpose they'll say Yes. If not they have no trouble saying an assertive No.

$ $ - Dollar sign for an S shows they are money minded. If they feel it's a good money deal for them they will say an assertive Yes. If they see it as a bad money deal for them, they will say an assertive No.

ʂ ʂ - Top is larger and more open than bottom shows they are open to discussing their future. They will say an assertive Yes if it's to talk about their future.

ʂ ʂ - Top is almost closed shows they are closed to discussing their future. They will say an assertive No if it's to talk about their future.

ʂ ʂ - Bottom is larger and more open than top shows they much prefer to discuss the past. They will say an assertive Yes if it's to talk about their past.

ʂ ʂ - Bottom is almost closed shows they are closed to discussing what happened in their past. They will say an assertive No if it's to talk about their past.

$$t \; t$$

The t-bar → t shows a person's:

> goal height (t-bar height on stem)

> goal enthusiasm (t-bar length & pressure)

The stem height ↑t shows a person's self evaluation.

t-bar height shows a person's goal line:

t t - t-bars high on the stem show they set their goals high. These are long term goals that take a long time to reach. They are willing to risk trying to achieve something they never tried before.

t *t* - t-bars in the middle of the stem show they set practical goals that take some work but they are sure they can reach. They need to know that investing their time will result in specific practical benefits to their life.

t *t* -t-bars that are low on the stem show they set low goals. These are short term goals of specific actions to take for a particular result. They want it to only take a short time to reach and want a sure result with no risk.

t-bar length & pressure show goal enthusiasm:

t *t* - Short t-bars show their enthusiasm to work on their goals only lasts a short time. Their enthusiasm runs out fast.

t *t* - Long t-bars show their enthusiasm to work on their goals lasts a long time. Their enthusiasm is like an inner cheerleader that keeps them going till the end.

t *t* - Light t-bar pressure shows they only have a limited amount of energy for their goals. They do best with goals that can be done sitting so they don't run out of energy.

t t - Heavy t-bar pressure shows they have strong physical energy that lasts a long time for their goals. They do best with goals that require at least some physical activity to put that energy to good use. Sitting still for long periods of time is not their style.

t - Heavy pressure with long t-bar is called willpower. They have strong will & energy to get their goals done.

t t - Overly long t-bars with heavy pressure that widens into a blunt end like a baseball bat, show they are willful and demanding. They impose their own goals on others, not concerned with what goals others have for themselves.

t stem height *t t* shows how they evaluate their work: (These meanings are also shown in d stems).

t t - Short t stem, called independent-t, shows they evaluate themselves on what they think is right. They are not concerned with getting praise or approval from others. They set their own standards which they have to meet for themselves.

t t - Tall t stem, called pride-t, shows they evaluate themselves on the pride they feel from praise received from others and the praise they give themselves about their work. They work as hard as they can to get as much praise as they can.

t_x T_x - Overly tall t stems (at least 3 times taller than their x-height) are called vanity-t or great-me-t. That shows they evaluate themselves on how much praise they get and they believe they deserve constant praise. When they don't get praise from others, they feel it's because they are too smart for others to comprehend and fully understand how truly great they are. Being convinced they constantly deserve high praise, they use that belief to constantly evaluate themselves high.

t t - Narrow or retraced t loops are called dignity-t. They evaluate themselves on how strictly they stick to what they have been taught is the right way to behave. If the loop is tall, their self evaluation also wants praise from others.

t t - Wide or inflated t loops are called sensitive-t. They evaluate themselves based on their own inflated self-expectations and their own inflated self-criticism. Some use their self criticism to improve their work and minimize the chances of getting criticized. Some wallow in self pity. Better to use this self-criticism for work improvement!

$\bar{\wedge}$ $\wedge$ - t stems separated into a tent shape $\wedge$ are called stubborn t. They stubbornly insist they are right even when facts show they're wrong. They evaluate themselves as right and protect themselves from being wrong by refusing to listen to what others have to say. The tent shape ∧ shows the walls they put up around themselves. Stubborn tents can also show up in the stem of ɑ← or ɖ←.

†Ť - Short sharp angles at the beginning of a letter are called temper tics. They show the person gets angry fast. Temper tics on the t-bar show they get angry easily while pursuing their goals.

t T - T-bars that slope up show they are optimistic about their goals. They believe if they work at them their goals will turn out fine. If the up-sloping t-bar is extra long /, they are ambitious and want the achievement of their goals noticed.

t T -T-bars that slope down show they have a pessimistic attitude that something bad will happen to their goals. They feel the need to protect their goals against criticism. To deflect criticism away from themselves, they often direct criticism at others.

ȣ T- Wavy t-bar shows they like to lighten the mood with humor. They use humor to keep from getting too stressed which helps them reach their goals.

T T - T-bar that is above the stem is called visionary-dreamer. Their goals often wander beyond what is practical or realistic into 'what if?'.

𝓣 𝑇 - Top bar on capital T that is neatly & simply attached to the stem, shows they are practical and have a direct approach to their goals.

𝓾 𝑢

u shows if a person will be up-front or cover-up their real feelings.

u open top takes information in and sends reply out.
u sides show how much information is wanted.
u bottom shows how the person reacts.

ʊ 𝑢- Wide top is fast to take information in and reply. Narrow top is slow letting it in and slow to reply.

𝑢 𝑈 - Tall or deep sides shows they want more information before they allow themselves to react. They want a deeper understanding first.

ᴜ ᴜ - Short or shallow sides shows they only want and only take in a small amount of information. They don't want to know more and may not be interested enough to have any feelings about it.

𝑢 𝑢 - Sides retraced shows they think their feelings but won't say them. They feel it's better not to talk than to say the wrong thing.

𝑢 𝑉- Angled bottoms shows they are up-front with their feelings. The angle shows their real feelings push right up out of their mouth. The angle also shows they want more details and are quick to criticize.

u - Narrow curved bottom with sides that open wider show bottom has a short reaction time with wide open top for wide open to giving their reaction. They are upfront with their real feelings.

u U - Narrow bottom with narrow sides shows they cover-up their real feelings by keeping their feelings to themselves.

u U - Moderately wide bottom shows they take time to consider other people's feelings before they react. They don't want to hurt other people's feelings.

⌣ ⊔ - Wide bottom and wide top show they are up-front with their real feelings. The wide bottom shows their feelings react for long time. And the wide top is wide open to say what's on their mind.

u ⊔ - Square bottom shows the reaction they show is what they feel is most practical and constructive for the situation.

⌣ - Wavy like a thread shows their reaction is to do what's easiest at the moment. The feelings they show are based on avoiding conflict and commitment.

U U - Clear & simple capitals show they have a direct manner. They are up-front with their feelings.

$\mathcal{U}$ $\mathcal{U}$ - Lead-in humps ↗$\mathcal{U}$ show they are careful, cautious, and self protective of their thoughts. They cover-up their real feelings.

$\mathcal{U}$ $\mathcal{U}$ - Lead-in loops that are small ↗$\mathcal{U}$ or flat ↗$\mathcal{U}$ show they are holding onto feelings of jealousy. They cover-up these jealous feelings and keep them inside.

$\mathcal{U}$ $\mathcal{U}$ - Lead-in large loops show they desire more responsibility. They want the chance to prove their abilities to others. They only show feelings they feel others will approve.

$\mathcal{U}$ $\mathcal{U}$ - Lead-in flourishes show they want to appear attractive. They only show the feelings that they believe are attractive to others.

v V

V shape with a sharp bottom in any letter (h m v) shows sharp thinking that quickly gets to the point of information. But v's have many possible shapes, not all have sharp bottoms. We'll use these shapes to show how people handle getting to the point of criticism said to them. Are they open to or resistant to criticism?

V V - Angle bottom v shows they have strong resistance to feeling bad from criticism. They quickly decide what is useful and what to dismiss.

ʊ ✓- Rounded bottom v shows they are open to hearing criticism. They easily accept it and easily feel bad from it. The wider the bottom the longer they feel the criticism. The wider the top the faster they react to try to resist feeling bad.

⟋⟍ V - Narrow v shows they keep resistant to criticism by only considering a narrow amount of it. If it doesn't match what they already think, they don't allow themselves to consider it.

⌣ ⋁ - Wide v shows they are wide open to criticism. They take it all in and consider it all. The width of the bottom is how long they hold onto it and how fast they react. Angle bottoms are quick to react and have a stronger resistance to criticism than curved bottoms.

Ⅴ ⱴ - Extra tall first stroke shows a resistance to taking in criticism. The tall first stroke shows they stay focused on their past accomplishments which they feel didn't get the attention they deserved. They resist considering new criticism because they feel that also won't acknowledge the attention they deserve.

Ⅴ Ⅴ- Second stroke longer and straight shows they resist taking in criticism. They stay focused on their future accomplishments which they feel will prove they are very capable. They believe their achievement will prove any criticism from others is not needed.

V ⋁ - Second stroke launches forward shows they resist criticism by launching themselves away from the situation the criticism came from. They take criticism as proof that it's time to leave that place.

⋃ V - One side crosses over the top shows they feel the need to protect themselves from criticism by not listening.

U ⋁ - Light pressure shows they have a low resistance to criticism and are immediately hurt by it. Their self protection is to take it in slowly and a little at a time to minimize how hurt they feel at once. They also try to appease the criticizer to lessen the hurt.

U V - Heavy pressure shows they have a strong outer resistance to criticism by quickly rejecting it and quickly confronting the criticizer. But what the person doesn't show is that inside they feel deeply hurt. They hold that deeply hurt feeling against the person who criticized them for a long time.

⋃ ⋃ - Mostly curves shows a gentle person who takes in all criticism and holds onto it, mulling it over and over. To feel better they change what was criticized to what pleases the other person so the critical feeling can be eased by hearing words of appreciation.

V V - Firm straight lines show a person is efficient and doesn't like to waste time. They only consider criticism they feel is practical and will benefit what they want to get done.

V V - Short sharp angles that begin a letter are called temper tics. The person with temper tics, if criticized, quickly resists criticism by getting angry fast.

WW

W has two sides.

The first side shows a person's own personality U.

The second side shows what they desire in others U.

$$U + U = W$$

W W - Sharp bottom angles in the first side show they are naturally competitive. The second bottom angle shows they also desire a competitive spirit in others. Both of these w-w want relationships with others who are as competitive as they are.

ᗕ ᗕ - Wide bottom curve shows the need for emotional support. The wider the first curve ᗕ the more emotional support they desire for themselves.

The wider the second curve ⋃ the more need for emotional support they desire in others.

w ⋃ - Simple lines with moderate width curved bottoms on the first side shows they are simply and naturally friendly. The same on the second side shows they desire others who are simply friendly without having extra needs.

W ⋃ - When both sides are equal width, they feel equally as capable and equally as important as others.

⋃ ⋁⋁ - First side wider shows that they focus more on themselves than on others. They are most concerned with their own needs and talking about themselves.

⋃ W - Second side wider shows that they feel the other person is most important. They are more concerned with the other person's needs and want to talk more about them than themselves.

W W - Narrow shows they hold back their feelings and thoughts from others.

W⋃ - The bottom side that is closest to the baseline, that's the person who needs to be the practical one. W shows they need to be the practical one. 𝒲 shows the other person needs to be the practical one.

ω ω - First side covered over on top shows they don't want to hear anything about themselves, but they're willing to hear about others.

ω ω - Second side covered over on top shows they don't want to hear about others but they do want to hear about themselves.

ω (ω - Both sides covered over on top show they are closed off to hearing what others say. They are often lonely but can't reach out.

W W - First stem much taller shows they want a lot of attention and love from others.

w W - Last stem much taller shows they have a lot of ambition and want others to notice their success.

W W - Center x shows they have a hard time trusting others.

W W - Clear & simple both sides show they are straight forward with others and want others to be straight forward with them.

𝒳 X

x has two lines:

Personality style line \ and Status wanted line /

→X← Crossing spot marks the status they want.

Personality style line \:

X X - Straight personality line \ shows they have a no nonsense personality. They are straight forward in what they want to do, and don't like wasting time. They put what's practical ahead of feelings.

X X - Curved personality line facing up ⌣ shows they have a gentle, flexible and giving personality. They openly share their thoughts and feelings, saying the right things at the right time. They want to be liked and like nurturing others.

𝘹 X - Curved personality line facing down ⌐ shows they have a gentle but cautious personality. They hold back what's on their mind until they feel it's safe to speak. They need time alone to think about their feelings and ideas.

𝘹 X - Wavy curve personality line ～ shows they have a strong sense of humor and are fun loving. They are also gentle, flexible, and nurturing. They like to keep others smiling.

Status wanted line / marks status they want →X←:

𝒳 X - Status wanted that crosses in the middle of the personality line like this →X shows they are comfortable with their current status. They are comfortable with the attention they receive and their ability to achieve what they want to do.

X Λ - Status wanted line crosses above the middle ↗X shows they place themselves at a higher, more important status than others. They feel above others, feel they should get more notice, and want to appear more prominent than others.

X X - Status wanted crosses below the middle→X shows they place themselves at a less noticeable status than others. They are not comfortable with attention. They are most comfortable being self reliant and avoiding interference by others.

𝒜𝒳 - Connected lines that don't require lifting the pen shows the person wants to be efficient and quick. They stick to their interests and don't seek any special attention or status.

Extra long reaches show extra status desired ✗↖:

✗✓ - Right side reaches extra high shows an extra strong desire to be noticed as highly successful. They want to prove their success and raise their status in the eyes of others.

✗ ⟩ - Left side starts extra high shows they hold extra strong feelings that in the past they didn't receive the extra notice they feel they deserved. They continue to reach for more attention for their past achievements to raise their status in the eyes of others.

✗ ⋀ - Right side pushes down extra long shows they want to be recognized as absolutely right. They are insistent and act over-confident as a way to prove they are right and raise their status in the eyes of others.

✗✗ - Left side pushes down extra long shows they desire a status where others notice their needs. They feel they didn't get the support for their needs that they needed in their past. They long for a status that shows them as important enough to get the support that they continue to long for.

Pressure shows if the person's driving force is from their personality \ or their status wanted / :

𝑥 X - Extra pressure on the personality line \ shows their main driving force comes from their personality, not their desired status.

𝑥 𝗑 - Extra pressure on the status line / shows their main driving force comes from their desired status, not their personality.

𝒴 Y

y = →U in body zone + leg in leg zone y↙
U in →y shows the person's openness to hear what others say.

ɣ ɣ - Narrow U shows the person is hesitant to listen to anything they don't already believe. They are uncomfortable considering anything they don't already accept as right and true. This is called narrow-minded.

𝑦 Y - Moderate-width U shows the person is open
to hear what others say and is comfortable talking about it. This is called open-minded.

u Y - Wide u shows the person is wide open to hearing and considering everything others say. They have wide open personal beliefs and easily believe things based on their feelings. This is called broad-minded because they easily consider a broader range of information than many consider reasonable.

Legs in ꜱy yꜱ show the person's will-try list.

(Also see g section. 'Go-getting' meanings of g legs also apply to y legs.)

y y - Narrow legs show the person has a narrow 'will-try list' to try new foods, activities, or friends. Their will-try list is limited to the few choices they already know they like. If they have a good reason, they may try something new.

y y - Moderate width legs show the person has an open will-try list to try new foods, activities, or friends. They like trying new tastes, interests, and having different kinds of friends.

y y - Wide width legs show the person has a wide open will-try list. They are excited to try new tastes, activities, and meet many different kinds of people.

y y - Legs with a tiny circle at the bottom show the person only trusts and associates with a tiny circle of people. This is called clannish. They also have only a tiny circle of foods and activities they will consider. They control everything tightly and have a very small will-try list.

y *y* - Legs pulled to the left show the person

longs for people, foods, and activities that gave them comfort in their past.

Leg length in y, or any leg, shows the length of time a person's determination to stay with a task will last:

y y - Short leg shows a short length of determination. They only stay with a task for a short time. They give up easily and fast.

y *y* - Moderate length leg (2x as long as the U) shows a

moderate length of determination. They will give a task a reasonable amount of time to accomplish it but won't like it lasting more than a day or week or possibly a month, unless they're highly interested or committed.

y *y* - Long length leg (2-3x as long as the U) shows

they have long determination for what they feel is important and their determination will last as long as it takes to get it done, even years.

y y - Extra long leg (more than 3x as long as the U) shows they have both long-lasting determination and an inner restlessness. This restlessness is called a desire for change. They are very quick to get up and go to other places or else to change their décor. When they feel stressed, they fantasize about being somewhere else. Still, they are a constant 'doer' and are always doing something. When they're not doing, that's when they feel their inner restlessness.

z Z

Z zips right into a person's personality by looking at the shape they choose for writing it.

z or *Z* - Cursive writers choose either a cursive *z* or a print *Z*. Those who choose the traditional cursive *z* show they like sticking to traditions they have learned work well for them. Cursive writers who choose print *Z* show they break with learned traditions for more straight forward actions. Those who use both cursive and print Z choose the one they prefer at that moment, whether feeling the pull of tradition or the push for straight forward action.

Ƶ Z - The extra line across the stem shows the person was taught this method to clearly distinguish Z from 2. This shows the person feels strongly about being precisely accurate in their communication with others.

ƶ Z - Straight lines show the person has a straight forward nature. They view their tasks with a straight line of steps to take. They also want to get straight to work and work straight through to get it done.

ƶ Z - Sharp angles show the person has a sharp insistent nature that gets straight to the point of what they have on their mind. They are sharp in how they speak and easily critical of what others are doing. They want things done their way and they get impatient with anything that stands in their way.

ƶ Ƈ - Curve in the lines shows the person has a cooperative nature. They are willing to bend their plan to consider other suggestions even after they have started. They are open to discuss the best way to proceed and change plans as they feel best suits new information.

2 - All curves show the person has a gentle, caring, and yielding nature. They always want to please others. They willingly give-in to other people's needs and choices.

1 - Narrow width shows the person has a narrow-minded nature. They stick with what they've already learned to be right and don't want to consider other possibilities.

2 - Moderate width shows the person has an open-minded nature. They have good common sense for what's practical. They are open to share what they know and willing to learn useful information from others.

3 - Wide width shows the person is broad-minded with a very tolerant nature. They are wide open to sharing their thoughts & feelings with others. They are also wide open in considering almost anything others have to say.

2 - Square looking shows the person has a logical precise nature. They like to figure out exact ways to construct things and follow precise plans.

ろ Z - Top bigger than bottom shows the person has a self-important nature. They think they should be seen as having a bigger importance than others. They are more concerned with appearing impressive than with the actions they take.

ろ Z - Smoothly written with a balanced top and bottom shows the person has the competence and confidence to get good results. They are more interested in doing it right than in proving themselves to others.

ろ Z - Light pressure shows they have a gentle nature. They avoid confrontation, choosing to be agreeable and please others as their way to accomplish what they want.

3 Z - Heavy pressure shows they have a forceful nature. Their strong will and strong physical energy push them to accomplish a lot. They will also quickly confront anyone trying to stop what they want to do.

Now you know clues to look for in

A-Z!